I Hold On

I Hold On
by Neeraja Krishnaswami
Paperback Edition

First Published in India in 2023 by

Inkfeathers Publishing
Vivek Vihar, New Delhi 110095
www.inkfeathers.com

ISBN 978-81-19483-60-0

I Hold On

a poet's introspection about life

Neeraja Krishnaswami

Inkfeathers Publishing
www.inkfeathers.com

to the three most important men in my life

(in the order of their coming into my life)

my father – who understood me and guided me
at every turn and bend.

my maternal grandfather – whose advice I remember
even to this day.

my husband – who made me feel worthy enough and
gave me confidence to walk with my head held high.

Author's Note

Hello everyone! I return as a solo author, venturing into this for the first time.

As you all know now, the title of the book says it all, but I want to share what inspired me to write this book and how this journey unfolded.

There were times, in the past decade, when I felt lost, helpless, and misunderstood. These emotions left me feeling worthless, breeding negativity and despair, incomprehensible to those around me.

All through the past decade, I was told not to worry or stress myself out. There were times when I thought life was not worth the time and effort. I encountered mighty mountainous lows throughout this timeline, and most of the people around me turned a blind eye to my sorrows. I was left introspecting on whether we get to choose our life or the situations that life throws at us.

At this juncture, I bring to you, 'Part 1: COLLAPSING,' which showcases my journey from year 2012 to year 2022.

Some of you might wonder or get curious here. How can one part of the book comprise of a decade's worth of feelings? I bet you are rummaging through the strands of your hair right now thinking about this.

Wait.

The second part, 'Part 2: AWAKENING', follows, showcasing life's ups and downs. Amidst despair, moments of beauty illuminated my path, reinforcing that life's worth is our creation.

I embarked on a journey of introspection and awakening in 2022 and 2023, exploring different facets of myself and society throughout the book. My poetry invites you to introspect, hoping you find answers as I did.

I hope this book's power transcends me, inspiring self-worth in you all. Even if one of you feel worthy of yourself after reading my poetry, I shall feel accomplished. I hope you enjoy reading 'I HOLD ON' as much as I enjoyed curating it.

Let the light within you show itself to the world. Live life. Embrace love. More power to you!

~ Neeraja Krishnaswami

Part 1
COLLAPSING

ABOUT THE INNER ME

‘It’s all about me
Or nothing.’

Or so is my inner mind believing!

‘It’s always all about you.
Or nothing.’

Say the characters in the story of my life.
Or is it them believing?

‘Isn’t it?’

Calls out my inner mind, which is an enemy to me—
A fact that is known to me
But now brushed under the carpet
In fear of being brandished by all and sundry.

Why do I feel threatened?
What is the barricade about?
'Break free and come clean.'
'Wash away the toxins till you breathe!'

It is my inner soul beckoning me.

'Why myriad of sounds create havoc volcanically?'
'What do I need when all my wants are fulfilled even though materialistically?'

'Why listen to the voice and keep reiterating?'
'Why expect more than what my heart is capable of carrying?'

Although these questions will always remain unanswered I know.
I know deep down that it is me renovating my soul, wholeheartedly!

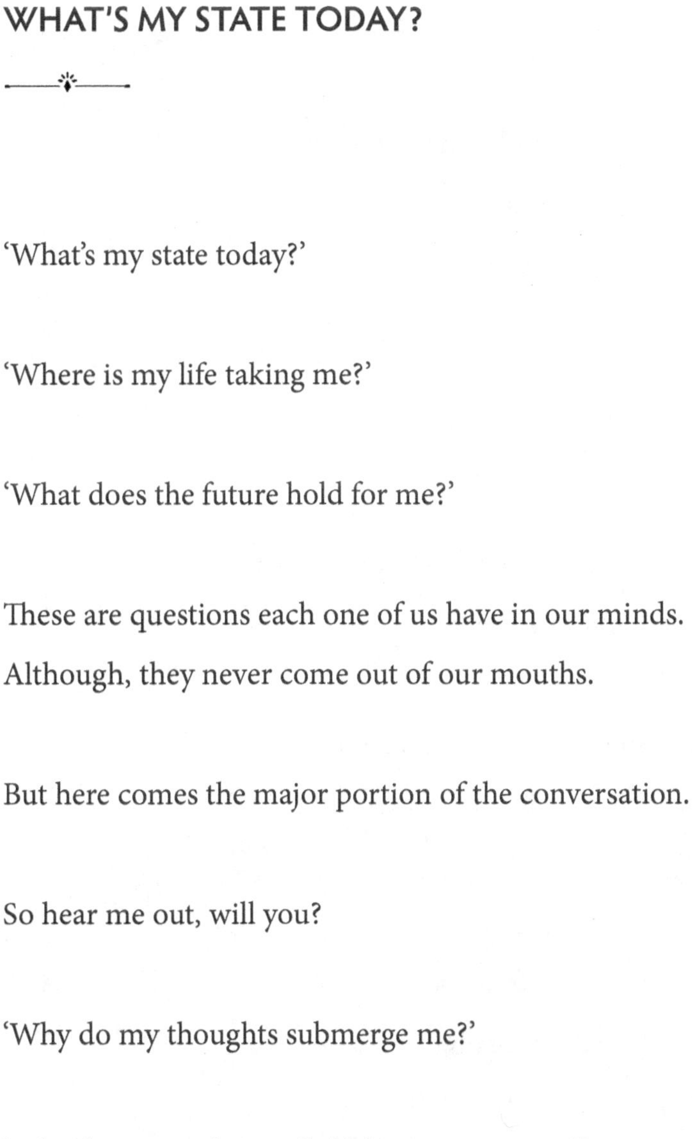

WHAT'S MY STATE TODAY?

'What's my state today?'

'Where is my life taking me?'

'What does the future hold for me?'

These are questions each one of us have in our minds. Although, they never come out of our mouths.

But here comes the major portion of the conversation.

So hear me out, will you?

'Why do my thoughts submerge me?'

'Why do you make me feel like an empty pot?'

'Why is my heart torn to the core?'

Does anyone—anybody—have answers
To these questions that rattle me
and give me sleepless nights
and intolerable days?

'The past decomposes,' they say.

'But what about the deep void in my heart—
that you left and ran away?'

'Neither to look back at me even once
Nor to see whether I was gleeful or in pain?'

But I lifted myself up,
And once the pen hit the paper,
All the contrived impossibilities hailed me
And told me that I am possible!

There was a time
When my existence
Seemed unimportant to me,
Never mind the crowds
Laughing at my weaknesses
Or celebrating my downfalls,
I would convince myself.

My wings, which I felt, were earlier cut off
To hamper my progress and dignity,
Have now been reinstated.

Now, I can gleefully
Share my joy with the world
That I'm no less than any other,
I am a free bird.

NO SOUL UNDERSTOOD ME

No soul understood me
Neither now nor in eternity
While I always strived for it, indefinitely.

My attempts were nothing short of a milestonic beauty
Which sadly went unnoticed by everybody.

Neither my crippling with fear
Nor my praying for the meagre
Was seen in totality.

It was seen with complacency,
Which I am now able to discern with utmost clarity.

No prayer proved my belief otherwise,
While all I prayed for, was sincerity.

Why should I go running to reach heights, is what I ask.
Why should I chase, when I know what's at the end of the tunnel,
Is what I want an answer for.

'Rhetorical questions give no answer,' say the winds forcefully.
'Hope is still there, don't give up,' says the afternoon Sun, calming me.

Asking the right questions
And looking for the right answers
Might go down well with somebody.
But it only confuses me.

I yearned to be part of people's lives,
Even if it was timely,
But what I got was nothing more than sheer brutality.

So now—I have no worries about now or eternity.

Living life my way is only the thing in my hands, it is the reality.

Nothing is in my control—all want to make me believe.

The yearning power has not been snatched away from me—I choose to believe.

Rather, it's your turn to yearn, for my compassion—I'd like to believe.

WHY DOES IT ALL HAVE TO RECUR?

Why do I feel unsure?
Why does it recur?

Why do I feel anxious?
Why does it recur?

Why do I feel restless?
Why does it recur?

Why do I feel so guilty?
So as to hold myself responsible
For everything wrong that happens
Within me and around me?
Why does this feeling recur?

Why do I feel the scathing scars of turmoil and distress
Disturbing me throughout the day

And snatching away a good night's sleep
So heartlessly?
Why does this feeling recur?
When every single feeling recurs
What is expected of me?

Why am I told
To keep calm?
To get along?
To march ahead?

Why am I told
To forget and forgive
When it's not palatable to me?

Where did all this begin
And when is all this going to end
Is my question.

But all I get
In the form of an answer
Is silence from the walls,
Is anger from the dusty brick and mortar,
Is an echo of dismay from the flowery garden
That bloomed, once upon a time.
All I see is my surroundings
Pouring out their frustration
In a manner most unexpected,
Sometimes through the regretful words of my near and dear
And sometimes through the words of remorse within my heart.

These are the questions that I ask
And sadly, don't find an answer to any
Despite being one out of the many
Who feel inquisitive.

All I feel in the end
Is plain agony and pain.

All that I'm left with
Is just the same question again and again.

Why does it all have to recur?
Just why?

THERE IS NO RESPITE

Gone with the wind,
Lost in the sands,
Tears moving downwards
Escaping my eyes,
Raindrops aligning themselves
Right on my dimples
And lingering on my face.

This is the ritual that follows
Each day and night.
And mind you—there is no respite!

I'm engulfed with thoughts that can't escape,
Still, I wander helter-skelter
To find that one ounce
Of warmth and truth
Amidst chills and lies.

The sight of a new leaf

Gives me peace and delight.

Now, all my feelings find

An opening through the perpetual emptiness

Where I lie dreaming awake

Amidst faith and might.

I AIN'T A WEAKLING

'What am I to get?'
'Where am I to get from?'
'Who is to give me?'
'Will anyone give me?'

'To get and give—is like to forget and forgive,' believe many.
'But all is a farce,' speak all and sundry.

Doomed and dessicated
Through illusions and allusions,
Seems the only way forward,
Whereas everything seems
To be in a standstill
Even though I courageously manoeuvre
Through thick and thin,
With kith and kin.

I know to get and give
I know, only too well,
To forget and forgive.
I do just that.

I ain't a weakling
Sitting on the sill
Or sifting through the blades of grass!

I just look through the blinding mirror
To catch hold of something
That's difficult to hold on to
And is way, way far apart.

IS THIS JUST ME?

There are a lot of things
one wishes for;

There are a lot of things
one dreams about.

When one's wish gets fulfilled,
Another's dream might have got squashed.

While one's dream would have turned into a reality,
Where another's wish would have never witnessed even the realms of positivity!

A wait for the new
While one sips the coffee brew;
All alongside the masked dew
With nothing more than a choice askew.

Fulfilling as it may seem
Desperate as we come across
Or is this just me?

Happiness is a warm gun.
And I cross off my unaccounted dreams like a to-do list,
with my hopes of the dew clearing,
Of the storms fading.

And us rewriting our story
With all the inner and outer energies well-wishing!

FALLING

It might be deep,
we might get drenched.

It might be shallow,
we might get cleansed.

It might be all against our nature
Many might make us fall.

Some might laugh at our misery,
while we might cry at their downfall.

Such is the might
of our existence,
while no one may realise
the extent of our fall.

THE EXTENT OF OUR FALL

We never seem to realise
Whether there are roses or thorns in our path.

We never seem to realise
Whether the roses are present at all
Or the thorns are submerged into the soil.

We never seem to realise
Whether the thorns are not thorns, really.

We never seem to realise
Whether they are the stones we need to step on,
The roads we need to carefully tread on,
To reach our goal.

We never seem to realise
Whether the seeds of creation need to be sown
In order to reap the benefits of bloom
In our path to glory and discovery.

We never seem to realise
What mistakes we did in the past
What lies in our present
What we are looking forward to
What we expect, of our future.

Ultimately, all this boils down
To the fact that we never realised
How speedily we were marching towards
A goal that was never defined,
A goal that that was only designed
To make us realise
The extent of our fall.

CIRCUMSTANCES

At times, we are faced with circumstances
One too many.

At times, we are forced to face
These circumstances.

What do we do then?

Do we get scared and run away?
Do we stand undeterred and look at the problem in its eye?

Some are made this way, to strive and achieve.
Some are made this way, to face and overcome.
Some are made this way, to deal with the issue and come out strong.

Such are the people whom we turn towards,
When we are faced with a challenging circumstance.

Such people give us the required teachings,
Make us strong enough to withstand the blows,
Keep us grounded, even when we are about to go astray.

Learnings we get from them
Keep us going in the right direction,
A direction that's right only for us at that point in time,
A step forward in the path that we initially intended to tread on.

Therefore, the time arrives, when we ourselves
Strive and achieve.

The time arrives, when we ourselves
Face and overcome.

The time arrives, when we ourselves
Deal with the circumstances and come out double strong.

DOWNPOUR OF EMOTIONS

Ever felt a downpour of emotions?
Ever yearned for even a tiny bit of reassurance?
Ever felt dejected at seeing your expectations not getting fulfilled?

Answers might be many,
but we may turn a blind eye,
Not wanting to face it.

Rigmaroles of negativity
And loopholes of deceit,
Are the two facets of
the emotions we encounter!

Not having any choice
We give in!

We give in to such pressures
while untiringly working
Towards taking positive strides,
Not realising how deep the puddle is!

Puddles may be many!

But nothing deters us
from raising our head
to see the world in great delight
to see the near and dear feel great joy
As we rise up ourselves!

DROWNING IN INSUFFICIENCIES

What does everyone think about me?
What do they opine about me?
Why do they always seem to judge me
Or point fingers at my incapacities?

Am I that incapable?
Am I that irresponsible?
Can I not be relied upon?
Do I always deceive everyone in my vicinity?

Is this just me asking these pertinent questions?
Or are these questions just a rhetoric inside my muddled head?

Are there answers to my beckoning at all?
The walls screech out in response.
Only the walls.

There is no human soul
That is patient enough to hear my ordeal
That is compassionate enough to keep a hand on my shoulder
Or giving a pat on my back and reassuring me.

Absolutely no one!

There, in that space and juncture
It is just me recounting my faults
And drowning in my insufficiencies!

Alas! Nothing more, nothing less.

DETACHED AND DERAILED

Full of irregularities
Full of insufficiencies
Full of potholes deep
Full of instances bereaved.

Stay calm, this is nothing.
Stay calm, or else you might not be able
To face what's in store!

Why should I?
Why should I keep calm
When the streets below my house
Are bustling in action?

Why should I?
Why should I keep calm
When the office space is so warm and welcoming
Yet the fact is that I feel detached and derailed
Whenever I step foot inside there?

Why am I expected
To be the best in everything
While the ones below me
Are reaping the benefits of my hard work and sincerity?
Why am I expected
To fulfil all my duties responsibly
While my superiors watch over me like a hawk
Without they themselves being accountable and duty bound?

In such scenarios
Isn't it fair of me to question their due diligence
And demand a position of equality
Amidst the fraternity?

When all the situations around me
Force me to withdraw
Force me to get derailed
Why shouldn't I become detached?

Why shouldn't I?
Just why?

REJECTION

Rejection.
The word in itself
Spreads an aura of negativity.

Rejection.
The thought in itself
Produces jitters within my entire body.

Rejection.
When do I reject myself?
When I look at other people doing better than me
Rise and shine beyond their capacity
And I am left to deal with mediocrity.

Rejection.
When do I get rejected?
When others view of me is that of an outcast.

Why so, one may ask.
If my success is like a deep throttled knife
To someone who is facing troubles
Then I am treated differently.

Alas! It is their viewpoint which I cannot change.
Alas! It is their thinking that I cannot convert.
All I can do is approach them carefully
And explain my situation calmly.

It is then in their best interest
And their level of acceptance for me
That will take them through
To the bright side of life.

It is said that grass on the other side
Is always greener
But it is for them to realise
That they'll lose a rare gem
Every time they reject me.

SACRIFICE

They know
That they are losing out on someone.

They know
That they are losing a rare gem.

They know
That they are losing me.

But do they realise
The value of a rare gem?

Do they realise
The value of me?

Do they realise
The depth of my emotions
Or the extent of my sorrows
When they throw me away?

All my sacrifices
Go in vain
Never letting anyone
Know how much their words
Shatter me, making a hole in my heart.

All my sacrifices
Are now out in the open
And it is for them to face
The wrath of it all
For, the one who dismisses
Never gets to see
The rise after the fall.

THIS TOO SHALL PASS

What's the matter?

Why do you cry?

Why do you feel low at times?

It isn't always possible

To keep a smiling face, you know.

So then, strive to reach a landmark,

To a place within you,

where you'd be

Wholesome

Undeterred

Unabashed

Understood

Determined.

I'm sure nothing will faze you there!

But what if life
and circumstances
Thrown at you,
Make you stagger
And impose it's beliefs and practices
On you?

What will you do then?
Where will you go?

What matters at that juncture is that
You're sure
That even though
Derailed
Detached
Mistook
Misunderstood,
Everything is okay
Everything is under your control.

And even though you might feel
Now is not the time for you,
There will come a time
When the world will be at your feet
And your word will be held in high regard.

You just need to
Keep reminding yourself
That this too shall pass.

Part 2
AWAKENING

SELF-DOUBT VS SELF-CARE

Why do we doubt ourselves?
Why do we doubt our capabilities?
And get drenched in the waters
Of our insufficiencies?

Why is not the question to be asked, say many.
And how do they say so, is something
That keeps us awake at night.

Still, we find no answers
Only to realise that these questions
Are repetitive, rhetoric and random
All thrown into one goblet of fire
With each one of us
Getting engulfed and burnt in this array,
To which there seems to be a start,
But no end.

We struggle,

We juggle,

We keep playing

Just to stay in the running,

Only to realise one day

That there is no avail,

Neither to our inquisition

Nor to our inhibition.

When we do realise this,

It is only poignant to note

That it is time now

For us to rise and shine

Without hurting anyone in the process;

For us to stop trembling and start mingling

With our own self.

This is the time
To realise how important self-care is
Rather than listen to those
Who share a toast and bask in joy
At our deflection.
This is the time to put ourselves
Into the shoes of our mature self
That self whom we see
As a reflection of our current doubtful self
And strive to achieve true goodness
Rather than false wealth and greatness.

LEARNINGS

Withstanding emotions is not something
That can be digested by many,
While enduring emotions is not something
That can be absorbed by all and sundry.

Not saying, 'You can do it.'
Not saying, 'This too shall pass.'
Never once reassuring me and saying, 'It is just a matter of time.'

Although I know deep in my heart
And yes, the fact has been ingrained in my blood
That no one is my teacher in this world.

I am my own teacher
I am the master of my own doings
And situations are the only experiences
That I derive my learning from.

Yes!

Learnings and more learnings

Guide me to take the middle path.

Yes!

They do guide me to take the path

One that is most non-controversial

One that is most non-judgemental

One that is filled with strength and focus

One that is filled with care and compassion

A path which I can tread on

With utmost confidence and clarity.

TO DREAM

Assuaging the mind,
Dissuading the mind,
Is some dream
Watching from far and wide.

Our inner senses try
To ebb the flow,
To calm the mind,
Failing each time!

We ride through the mines
And sail through the tides
Every single time!

Our eyes become moist
When we succumb to wishes.

Yet, none can stop us
From walking towards
Our dreams so sublime!
Dreaming is not our aim,
Neither our passion.

Yet, we carry each dream
In our hearts
With love and light.

Freeing ourselves from the crossroads
Climbing out from the potholes,
We dare to dream!

And inspire the onlookers
To tread on the path
That is known best to them!

To fly like the carefree birds,
To sail through the seas,
To calm the storms inside them,
To dare to dream!

TO BE KIND

Kindness is something we wish for,
Kindness, at times, is something we crave for.

All of the world sees us
as kind-hearted souls,
For never have we once
Said or done otherwise!

Then why now has our course changed
Is something we ourselves wonder!

The path that we have always tread on
Has now died a million deaths!

We feel that all hope is lost;
We feel all of the time has betrayed us,
And there comes a time
Where we feel as nothing in the world
Belongs to us!

There are some who feel the same as us
Sorrowful, dejected, and numb.

Yet, there are some who still believe in us
For we are souls who are
Joyous, motivated, and sensitive.

Here comes our internal bliss
When we put our ancestors' teachings
Into play!

These teachings give us a reason
To live as humans
Where we learn
That our blunders are as ordinary as the rest.

Some might want to deter us
Go against us;
Yet our kindness foils their ploy!

Here, we get going
Taking all moments in our stride!
Kindness is our choice
Kindness is our belief
Where all realise
That we are preachers of a kind;
That this is our moment of positive pride!

RISING

All our days might be green
All our nights black!

All our months might be good
All our years might be crazy!

None of us do anything deliberately
While others might deliberate
On our rise!

Rising always comes after a fall,
Say everyone!

But why did we fall
Or why is anyone in the wrong,
Is a question everyone ask without fail,
But seldom does anyone dare to answer!

Rising always comes after a fall,
Say everyone!
But, every rise comes with a price,
Say others!

What is that price,
Which one needs to pay,
To rise above everyone?

What is that price,
Which one needs to pay,
To stay perched at the top?

What is that price,
That one needs to keep paying,
To dissuade others
From competing or combating?

Even if we extend an olive branch,
Some might take it as our selfishness,
While the true ones would come to know
How selfless we are!

The price paid to stay perched at the top
Is the secret we endure.

Everyone's astounded by our rise,
But now, the tables have turned.

None ask us how we maintain our balance,
Nor do they deliberate on on our rise.

They only fear our blaring gaze
And seldom want to come
In our line of sight.

MESSENGERS FROM THE SILVER STARS

When you feel people are looking, why do you feel so?
You feel so, for sprouts of doubt
have been deeply ingrained
In your blood.

The messengers from the silver stars
Beckon you to grow and feel your internal growing battles
Which seem like they'd never end.
The full stop seems to have vanished into thin air.

Viewing yourself from a different prism
And seeing yourself through unknown eyes
Give you the courage and the drive
To do better and better,
Maybe not a class apart
But nonetheless, a mix of all at heart!

All in all,
Helping you climb the ladder
Slowly and steadily,
Taking you a notch higher,
Where struggles and strife are put into the back-burner
And greetings and fondlings make for more cheer!

COUNT YOUR BLESSINGS

Just when we want acceptance
We receive rejection.

Just when we crave for popularity
We go unrecognised.

Just when we feel the need for something
Something else gets in the way.

With so many negatives around us
Which we still swim through
We always strive
To reach out to
That one ounce of positivity
Which looks like a ray of hope
Amidst a whole haystack
Of pins and needles.

Not to forget,

That one rotten mango

Can spoil a whole crate of them,

But why do we need to be

That rotten mango,

We question ourself.

And when no word comes across to quench our inquisitiveness,

We resort to thinking more

Ruminating more

Analysing more.

Somewhere here,

We get lost into the pool

Of thoughts, moods, and emotions,

Get muddled in our head

With more than what we can take or grasp

And cry like a baby when

We aren't able to reach the pinnacle

Which we set for ourselves!

So why set boundaries?
Why keep targets?
These are good
For short term planning
But we can never depend on these
In the long run
As we don't know to foresee the future
As we don't know what awaits us at the end of the dark tunnel
As we don't know whether we'll live today or
Go on forever tomorrow.

So all that we can conclude is
Live for today
Be thankful for what you've got now
And count your blessings till they last.

WHEN I WAS A CHILD

When I was a child,
I felt as if there was no end to happiness.

When I was a child,
I felt there was no need to worry.

When I was a child,
I felt as though I could conquer the world.

When I was a child,
I felt that everything was in my capacity.

Little did I know,
That life's mysteries were about to unfold.

Life's mysteries did unfold,
In a manner that none could behold.

Life's mysteries did unfold,
Through a meadow of yearnings
And through the stillness of grief.

The morning dew,
The crisp breeze
And the dandelion-filled yard
Helped to cope in ways distantly close.

The jagged black rocks
Helped me decipher the negative space,
Where I did discover ordinary happiness
And whispers of dreams forgotten.

Although an adult now,
I still feel that I am a child.

I still feel that I am a child,
Waiting to reach the horizon,
Waiting to reach the sky.

Waiting to reach the sky,
And tell the world beneath,
That hey!
I'm coming now,
I'm coming now
To take what's lawfully mine,
And yes, I'll make sure I shine.

LIVE, LOVE, LAUGH

Situations arise
When one misses a step
When one falls down
When one goes haywire.

Living becomes a burden
On oneself
Making easy pathways
Seem tough.

Situations arise
When one wishes to love
When one wants to be loved
When one sees no exit
From the now except to follow
The path of love.

Love is a feeling, say some
Love does not exist, say others
A quarrel engulfs both the factions,
While the spectators realise
The true meaning of love
Just by observing the two sides of love
Getting caught in disengaging discussions,
Who failed to understand even now!

A situation arose
A light laugh escaped one
While another chuckled.

All heads, including the factions,
Turned toward that duo
One still had a twinkle in his eyes,
And the second one's lips curved into a smile
Neither of the two
failing to praise the sight,
That all were astounded.

One eased the turmoil;

The other offered to bring in joy

For they were the ones

To laugh at the sight,

Rather than cry.

CALM, SURE, STRONG, AND DAUNTLESS!

Glad when fine;
Strong when we shine.
Dauntless when things get hazy;
Upturned when things get cosy.

Yet, we remain calm when in agony,
And sure when we cry.
Yet, we seem fine when things get cosy
And shine when things get hazy.

Here, we witness life turning upside-down,
Life getting nowhere;
While we have everything,
Where we need not anything;
While we needn't worry,
Even when we battle injury.

Calmness is key
Say all and sundry;
Let the moment pass
We hear from everybody.

Still we cry,
When we see our near and dear in agony and pain,
While we mask our own internal battles
Without any shame!

Yes, we are
No, we're not;
Goes the phrase, when we try to justify,
And we fail each time while trying to simplify!

Enough is enough!
Our heart says.
Keep going!
Our mind says.

And yet again,
We get caught in this whirlwind
Of thoughts, actions, and impressions alike,
Carrying bliss and harmony in our hearts,
For a world so mystified!

Calm when in agony;
Sure when we cry;
Glad when fine;
Strong when we shine!

I HOLD ON

Sometimes, my mind seems
Like an empty palace of dreams
Lost in the expanse of
A delusion.

In other times, my mind seems
Like it's carrying a load full of pins and needles,
Playing on the hypotenuse of
An illusion.

Gone are the nights
Where I'll cry
Before falling asleep.

Gone are the days
Where my mindset wanders
Into the matters of the world.

Still, there are times
When I feel the need of
Kind words from a stranger.

Or, where wanting to hear
Words of solace from a dear one
Seems my only escape.

When neither happens,
I see my life
Dissolving like a sandcastle by the sea.

When neither happens,
I see my life
As though it was never meant to be.

Still, I don't let go!
I hold on tight.

I hold on to the chains and shackles
Around my mind
With all my might.

I hold on

Till my heart bleeds

And tears escape my eye.

Now, I hear a voice inside my head,

Walking through the aftermath

And beautifying my bed.

It's time to sleep again

After bidding goodbyes

Till the dawn of a new day arises

And the thought of

A new moment

A new call at the beck of it all

Keeps me dreaming of what would be

My happily ever after.

BECAUSE THERE'S NOTHING CALLED FOREVER

How does it matter
If the train leaves?

How does it matter
If the strands break away?

How does it matter
If the life of our dear ones is at stake?

How does it matter
If we the emptiness within us
Paves way for greater potholes in our relationships?

We can definitely
Catch the next train
Weave another strand.

But we cannot defy
The laws of distress and incapacity.

We cannot deny
That the room once full
with echoing laughter and jokes
is now empty and there's a void.

A void that will get filled with time.

Time immemorial, we know that
Time and tide waits for no man.
And man, these days
Hankers after lost ties
Without realising that
There are strands
Left incomplete in a relationship of any kind.

It's time to tie those loose ends
And realise who cares and who does not.

Not saying caring is a dilemma,
It is a rarity found often
Within dungeons and deep seas,
Or within folded pages of a little diary.
It's time.
It's time we know what's in store for us next.
Even if we don't come to know,
Never mind.

Enjoy the simplicity
The peace and calm
The quiet and still
The moon and the sun
The days and the nights
While it all lasts
While we last.

Because there's nothing
Called forever!

ONLY I, TRULY KNOW

Today, I feel different.

Today, I feel wanted.

Today, I feel brilliant.

Today, I feel loved.

Not like I was being viewed differently, in the past.

But today, something has changed.

My view about myself

Has undergone a transformation.

Is this due to

Some people exiting my life?

Or is this due to new ones entering my life?

It's a bit of both, I choose to believe.

Only I, truly know
That yesterday, the words trembled on my lips,
That yesterday, my heart's chambers were locked stiff,
And I had nowhere to go.

Only I, truly know
That today, after all these years,
You land up in my life,
In the most unexpected of ways,
Bringing hope and sunshine into my days,
Overthrowing the plight of lies,
And the moths of deceit,
That used to cloud my nights
Like dancing shadows on the wall.

Today, I'm locking the doors to my past,
Freeing myself
Of all the guilt and misery,
Of all the disdain and treachery,
Embracing what lies ahead of me,
Without force, noise, and irrationality,
With grace, poise, and humility.

Life is a cosmic breeze
And songbirds flutter inside my heart
And only I, truly know
That today, I am ready to face
All that is laid in my way.

All that I ask for is
Love and care,
Strength and hope,
Honesty and understanding,
And I promise to overcome everything
With you by my side,
Basking in hay.

IN BLIND TRUST AND FAITH

There were times when I've felt

That I could trust no one.

There were times when I've felt

That no one, absolutely no one, was worthy of my trust.

There were times I sat wondering

As to—whom do I trust?

There were times I sat thinking

As to—what if they broke my trust?

Just when all these doubts

Consumed my brain

And punched a hole in my heart,

You came.

You came and told me
That life is beautiful.

You told me that life is worth living
And willed to take me aboard.

You helped me make my choices
And helped me while I was in doom.

You never ever thought much
While holding my hand
And walking with me
In this odyssey called Life.

I started believing in trust and faith
Due to you entering my life
And not leaving, but staying.

Now I trust you completely,
While also being cautious
And not succumbing to anyone and everyone
In blind trust and faith.

WHAT MORE COULD I HAVE ASKED FOR?

Once upon a time
I was a nobody.

Once upon a time
I was not cared for.

Once upon a time
I never believed in destiny.

I never believed
Someone was out there,
Waiting for me to reach out.

Then, there came a day
When that someone was waiting for me.

I realised that he was waiting for me
When he said our destinies were walking the same path.

Neither did anyone
All these years
Share his joys
Nor did anyone
All these years
Understand my pain.

When our paths crossed, one fine day
We gelled so well,
As though we knew each other
For years.

He understood my pain.
I could see where he came from.

We both had experienced lows
Of types that differed in ways too many.

Yet, we connected.

We laughed so hard
Till the point of tears escaping my eye,
But he was right beside me,
Wanting to treasure even that lone tear,
Which he felt was a precious pearl
Out of an oyster shell.

His joys found a home within me.
My sorrows carved a place within his heart.

What more could I have asked for?

I FEEL AT HOME

Be it at home
Or outside of home.

Be it in our nation
Or outside our nation.

What I feel
What I want
What I speak

What I sense
What I show
What I imbibe

What I create
What I spill
What I gather

What might seem as my reflection
What might seem as my introspection
What might seem as my deflection

All of it boils down
To my sense of longing
For peaceful paths
Of desired meanings
For serene waters
Of grateful giving!

I want all of it
Yet, I aspire to settle into
Tranquil surroundings
For at this very place
I feel at home.

NOTHING BUT BLESSED

My thoughts emerge from various things, spaces, and situations, I agree;
My words lead to varïous opinions, judgements, and criticisms, I know;

I feel all are drifting away,
with me watching on helplessly as they surpass me;

Only to realise
that today, I stand here with nothing,
that today, I'll go home empty handed.

I know this only too well
that I carry in my heart a million wounds;

Yet, I am truly blessed
to be an inhabitant of an ocean,
filled with goodness and harmony.

Yet, I am truly blessed
To be a recipient of the love,
from all those around me.

Yet, I am truly blessed
To be one of a kind and share the joys
I feel within me.

INTROSPECTING ABOUT LIFE

Oh, wait.
Shall we speak about Life?
Or is it worthwhile to rather introspect on it?

Give me a hearing, will you?

So.
LIFE.

Well, it's said that Life
Begins the day one is born
And ends the day one reaches
His or her Heavenly Abode.

True that.

But here are my arguments
In favour of why Life
Is worth living
Or rather why is Life
Worth the introspection.

Life is simple, yet complicated
Not a merry-go-round
Where we play around with no avail.

Life is, sometimes, an umbrella of nightmares
Which we need to keep going along with
In order to reach our desired destination.

Life is a bundle of mundane musings
Which are only answered by echoes
In the mystic allure of spirited darkness.

We can't choose our Life
It chooses us
And we have no other option
But to embrace the plethora of darkness
And tread on the abundance of brightness
All of which encompasses Life.

Life and health go hand in hand
And life is worth living
If we are healthy, not wealthy.

Life is always about being trustworthy
Yet, it is noteworthy
That we need to tread on each step cautiously
And take each action seriously.

For if not taken so,
There might come a time
Where the grey skies
May cause manic mayhem
and the lubricated windows to heaven
Might swing open.

In order to avoid risky circumstances
Life is worth the wait
Life can even be endured
With the slightest rays
Of hope amid fear
Of care amid plight
Of composure amid displeasure
Of serenity amid adversity.

So yes, what do you think?

Is life worth the time and introspection?

I leave you to find out for yourself.

ACKNOWLEDGEMENTS

Firstly, I thank all my language teachers throughout my school and college life for instilling the habit of reading and writing in me. Although I was out of touch with language and literature all through my work life, I am grateful to you all for unknowingly inspiring me to make the move towards language and literature once again.

I would like to thank Uma Bokil (the then Publishing Manager and my first supervisor at Inkfeathers Publishing) and Sagar Kumar Bharadwaj (the co-founder of Inkfeathers Publishing and my current supervisor) for all the support, able guidance, and handholding throughout the process without even thinking once that I was a newbie in this field.

A huge bow of gratitude from me to the entire Inkfeathers Publishing family for providing the platform I required to curate my first ever solo poetry book. Without all of your support and continued encouragement, I wouldn't have been able to get this far.

And last but not the least, I thank my mother, my husband and my entire extended family and my friends and acquaintances who believed wholeheartedly that I would execute this project and encouraged me to bring this book out to you all.

ABOUT THE AUTHOR

A Tamilian by birth and a Mumbaikar at heart, Neeraja Krishnaswami is a postgraduate in Business Management, a certified HR professional, a fiction and non-fiction blogger, a co-author in anthologies, and an internationally published author and book reviewer. She has recently opened her own proprietary concern, RahNee Interior and Architectural Design Consulting, to further her husband's dream of designing exquisite homes and office spaces.

Moreover, her motto is to spread awareness about social issues, and she feels that the mental health of all is prime, and everyone must take out some time from their busy schedule to spread awareness about healthy and peaceful living in whatever manner possible.

Apart from reading and writing, her hobbies are singing, painting, and landscape photography.

You can find her writings and artwork through her two Instagram handles: @neerajak_94 and @nkay.reads.writes.sings.

We love creating beautiful books for you!

Come be a part of our ever-growing community of authors.
Grow, write, and publish with us!

Connect with us on socials.
We'd love to hear from you!

@Inkfeathers Publishing

www.ingramcontent.com/pod-product-compliance
Lightning Source LLC
LaVergne TN
LVHW041123150826
845673LV00007B/2164

* 9 7 8 8 1 1 9 4 8 3 6 0 0 *